# Blues Hanon

Blues Hanon

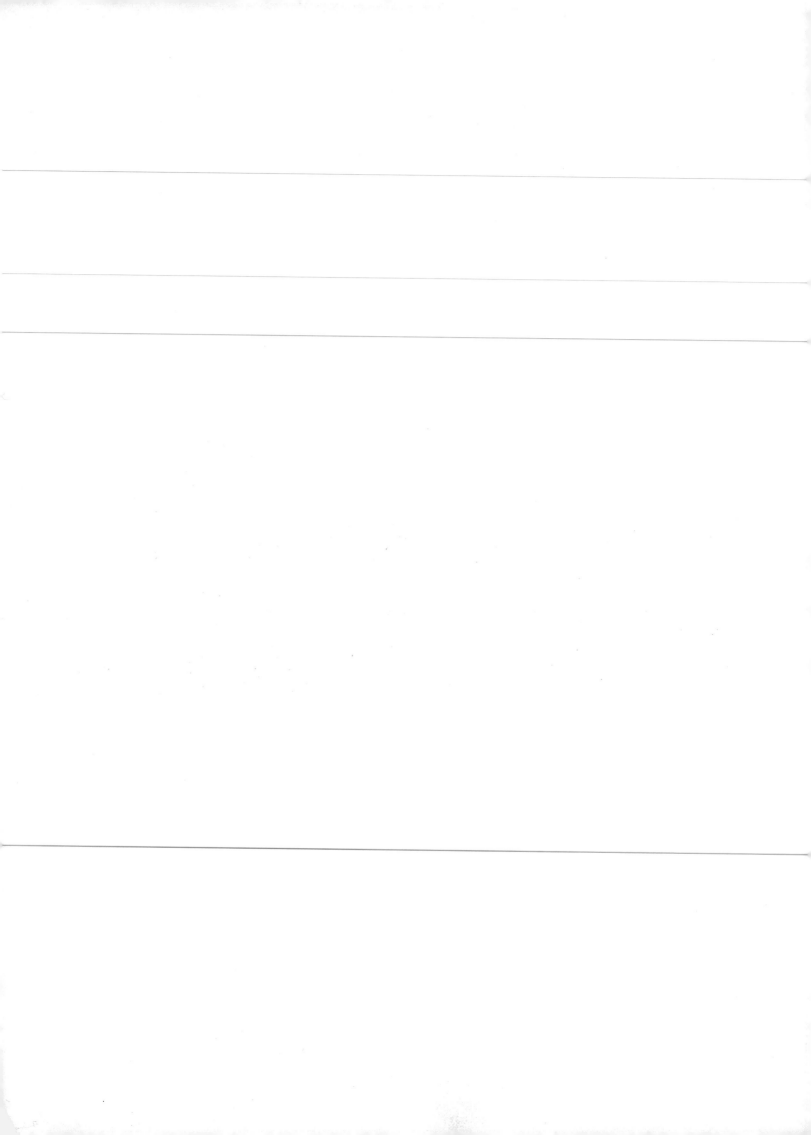

# Blues Hanon

by Leo Alfassy

**Amsco Music Publishing Company**
New York · London · Tokyo · Sydney · Cologne

Edited by: Brenda Murphy
Cover illustration by: Tom De Jong
Cover design by: Werner Jurgeleit

edcba

International Standard Book Number: 0-8256-2224-7

Distributed throughout the world by Music Sales Corporation:

33 West 60th Street, New York 10023
78 Newman Street, London W1P 3LA
4-26-22 Jingumae, Shibuya-ku, Tokyo 150
27 Clarendon Street, Artarmon, Sydney NSW 2064
Kölner Strasse 199, D-5000, Cologne 90

# Contents

# Introduction

The blues, a primal formal structure in American popular music, is perhaps the most significant contribution of blacks to the musical heritage of this country. It had a profound impact on the development of jazz and permeated a good deal of concert music as well.

Although a product of black culture, the blues is an amalgamation of Afro-American and European traditions. It makes use of elements of harmony and form from European musical common practice, being essentially a strophic song set to three-line stanzas. But the African influence is significant in many ways: 1) the melodic line consists of mostly descending phrases; 2) the scales contain "blue" notes (flat sevenths, thirds, and fifths); 3) the voice has a special open quality, employing glissandos, melismata, and falsettos; 4) there is a polyrhythmic interplay between the voice and the accompaniment.

The emergence of the blues and the closely related boogie-woogie as identifiable entities is very difficult to determine, mainly because they were kept alive by oral tradition. Around 1900, when musicology was in its infancy, very few ethnomusicologists realized that the musical heritage of the nonwestern world merited scientific research. We must rely on the memory of the very few musicians still living and other chroniclers, whose vague recollections offer little accurate information about the first steps of this indigenous American art form.

The principal sources of the blues were Negro spirituals and work songs, mainly the hollers sung in the levee camps along the southern rivers and the fields. Field hollers were unaccompanied songs in free rhythm, characterized by their wailing sound, very similar to the songs of the farmers in northwest Africa. They were "complaints" against difficult working conditions, the powerful landlord, love problems, etc. Gradually, the free-rhythmed hollers evolved into songs with stronger metric accents and more precise formal structure. But the blues still remained the most personal expression of the depressed, dissatisfied, melancholic, and rootless black people of the South.

From the turn of the century to the 1920s, when the agricultural South was gradually industrialized and when itinerant black workers found jobs in the sordid slums of the northern and midwestern cities, the rural vocal blues was transformed into an instrumental urban composition with a more dance-like character. Many itinerant pianists played the blues for endless hours in dark juke joints, rent house parties, and barrelhouses (cheap drinking establishments with barrels stacked along the walls for sitting purposes and a dirt floor for dancing). In this environment was created the barrelhouse blues style. It was a quite rude pianistic language, created by self-taught musicians and adapted to the rough audience and to the mechanical conditions of the dilapidated instruments.

In the early 1920s, after the closing of the red district in New Orleans, many black musicians moved north along the Mississippi River and created new jazz centers, especially in Kansas City, Memphis, St.Louis, and Chicago. It was in Chicago that a new generation of pianists with musical schooling developed a richer harmonic and stylistic vocabulary, introducing the blues into more respectable establishments and the recording studios.

The black composer W.C. Handy played an important role in the development of the blues. He was the first orchestrator who collected melodies from the performers he heard around him, then harmonized and published them in the early 1910s. As a result, a new generation of young jazz musicians became familiar with the blues chord sequences, improvised on them, and created new melodies.

In 1920, the first blues record by a black vocalist appeared, followed by thousands of "race" records intended exclusively for black customers. By the mid-1920s, the blues reached a mixed audience, becoming a popular dance form which was no longer associated with depression and lamentation. Instrumental blues appeared in a variety of tempos and characters, and to a musician the expression "playing the blues" meant improvising on a succession of twelve-bar "choruses" and a sequence of chords.

The second half of the 1940s saw the development of a more sophisticated style, especially after the introduction of electrically amplified instruments in the jazz band. The bebop, a progressive jazz style of this period, was strongly influenced by the blues tradition.

The 1950s witnessed the emergence of "rhythm and blues," which is the progenitor of rock 'n roll. Even today the talent of a jazz musician is judged by his ability to extemporize spontaneously within this fundamental jazz form, which accounts for about one third of all popular music.

The next section explains the characteristic features of the blues in relation to the basic elements of music. This is followed by thirty-three practical exercises, each dealing with a specific technical problem for the left or right hand. In order to acquire an absolute independence of hands, it is necessary to practice each hand separately. This should be done in a slow tempo and without the use of the right pedal. Instead, the student can keep a steady tempo by tapping the beat with his right foot.

# Elements of Blues Style

## Melody

The blues began as a lamentory chant with irregular phrase structure and free rhythm. Gradually, it developed into a simple repetitious twelve-bar melody, consisting of three brooding descending phrases with a driving rhythmic accompaniment. Each musical phrase corresponds to one line of the three-line blues stanza, with an instrumental interlude.

Often one or more initial eighth notes precede the phrases in the form of an upbeat.

In order to follow the changing harmony, the musical phrases can be altered chromatically (a), or transposed to another pitch above or below (b).

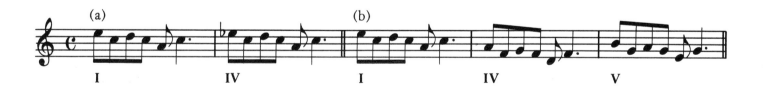

The melodic line of the blues cannot be judged in the same way as that of a classical piece, or even in the same way as another kind of popular melody. It furnishes only the framework for creative improvisations and ceaseless embellishments; the performer being more or less the spontaneous composer.

# Harmony and Form

The harmonic and formal structures of the blues and the boogie are the same. Every composition consists of a succession of twelve-bar sections called "choruses," each section containing an identical harmonic pattern. This pattern is based on the triads built over the first (tonic), fourth (subdominant), and fifth (dominant) degrees of the scale. Here is the formal and harmonic structure of a typical blues or boogie in the key of C.

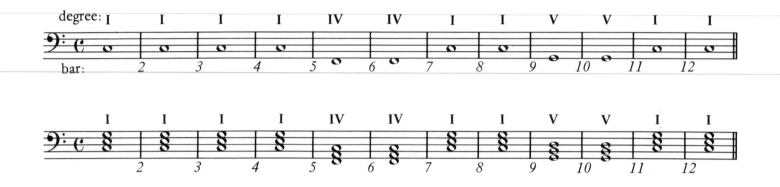

Sometimes the tonic triads of measures 2 and 10 are replaced by the subdominant triad or a minor seventh chord.

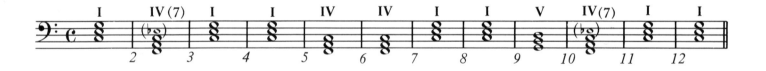

There are many exceptions to this basic harmonic pattern. The great performers of blues and boogie use sophisticated chords, tone clusters, and strikingly original progressions within this fundamental framework. Here is a modern version of the blues (or boogie) form.

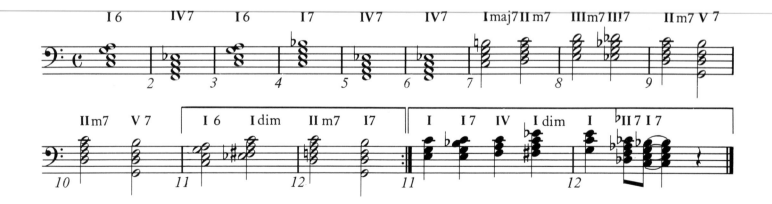

# Bass Line

The development of a good left-hand technique is essential in blues playing because of the twofold importance of the bass line: as a harmonic support, and as a replacement for the rhythm section of a band. A simple bass figure can consist of the repetition of open fifths or chords.

The bass line can also consist of the so-called "walking bass" (notes "walking" up and down a scale or in broken chords), probably derived from the common bass patterns of jazz bassists.

Here are some other typical bass figures.

# Blue Notes and Scales

The melodic line often contains features typical of the blues, namely the so-called "blue" notes. These are notes, particularly the third, fifth, and seventh degrees of the scale, whose intonation lies *between* the major and minor pitches. (For practical purposes, these degrees are flatted by a semitone.) In blues singing, these notes could be easily "bent" or "glided" by the singer or played on the guitar, the most important instrument for blues accompaniment. In order to imitate the blue notes, which were impossible to play on a keyboard instrument, the blues pianists had to develop a special technique of embellishments consisting of grace notes and slides.

Although most blues melodies are based on the major scale, some use other scales such as tonal or semitonal pentatonic scales, or "blues scales" containing the blue notes. Tonal pentatonic scales consist of only five notes and include no semitones.

The last inversion of the above example is quite often used in blues, especially in a descending line.
Semitonal pentatonic scales include semitones.

The blues scale adds blue notes to the major scale but omits the second, sixth, and major seventh degrees.

Sometimes blues pianists use a minor triad in the right hand and a major triad in the left hand simultaneously.

# Meter and Tempo

The meter of the blues, like most jazz music, is **C** (common). Often the second and fourth beats of the bar (backbeats) are heavily accentuated. Some pieces are in $\frac{6}{8}$ or $\frac{12}{8}$ meters, partly under the influence of gospel songs.

The blues and the boogie-woogie have much in common: the formal structure, the chordal sequence, and some bass figures. But there are certain differences, two of them being the tempo and the dynamics. Since the blues is originally a song of lamentation describing a life close to the bone, it is usually in a slow tempo and on a medium dynamic level. On the other hand, the boogie is a heavily percussive piano style with great rhythmic vitality. It is played in a fast tempo on a quite high dynamic level.

# Exercises

**1.**

**2.**

**3.**

**4.**

## Syncopation

The next exercise introduces a very important device in jazz, syncopation. Syncopation is, generally speaking, any deliberate displacement of the natural accent from a strong to a weak beat. In western music, every bar contains strong and weak beats. In $\frac{4}{4}$ meter, the first and third beats are strong; in $\frac{3}{4}$ meter, only the first. Example (a) shows the natural accents in $\frac{4}{4}$ and $\frac{3}{4}$ meters. Example (b) illustrates the displacement of these accents.

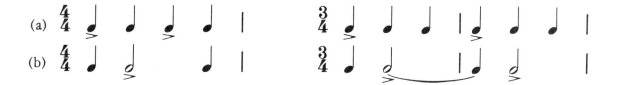

Jazz especially uses syncopations on shorter time values (eighth and sixteenth notes), which creates a complete imbalance in the listener's feeling of rhythmic security and excitement.

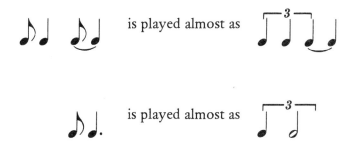

In classical music, the proper way to perform a syncopation is to accentuate it heavily. The jazzman softens these accents by prolonging the value of the shorter note and playing it almost as long as the syncopated note. For instance:

17

**5.**

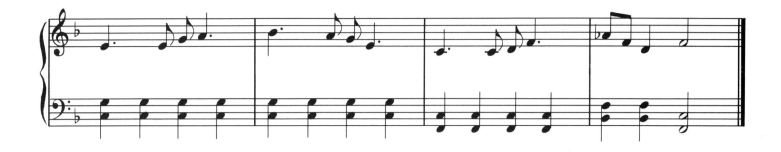

### Parallel Thirds and Sixths (Right Hand)

Exercises 6 through 9 deal with thirds; exercises 11 through 13 deal with sixths in the right hand. Parallel thirds and sixths are difficult to perform evenly; the two component keys must be struck precisely together. I recommend the major and minor scales as preparatory introduction to these exercises.

**6.**

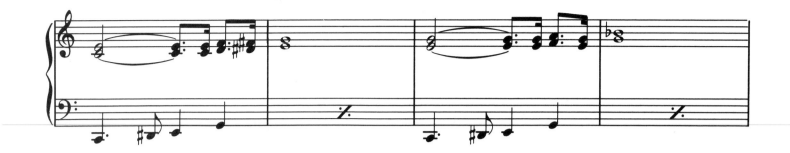

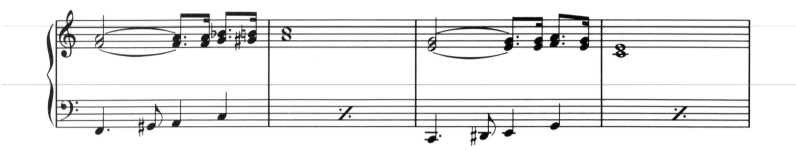

**7.**

**8.**

**9.**

### Blue Notes

The next exercise introduces blue notes. As explained previously, the blue notes occur mostly on the third, fifth, and seventh degrees of the scale, which are flatted. Often one hand plays a major triad while the other one plays a minor chord. This is, of course, done purposely.

**10.**

25

**11.**

**12.**

**13.**

**Grace Notes**

In classical music, the time value of a grace note (note printed in small type) must be subtracted from that of the preceding or following notes. In the interpretation of blues, the value of the grace note is extremely short—in other words, the grace note and the adjacent note are played almost simultaneously *on* the beat. This extremely short value is achieved through the sliding of the same finger from a black to a white key on the keyboard.

Because it is impossible to slide with the same finger from one white to another white key, or from a white to a black key, two fingers are necessary to perform the grace note and the adjacent note.

To create an even greater illusion of guitar playing, the blues pianist often strikes simultaneously two notes situated a semitone apart (a). The agglomeration of a few semitones in the same chord, called "tone cluster," adds more excitement to the music (b).

**14.**

**15.**

As mentioned before, a jazz musician softens syncopated and dotted notes. In the next exercise, the dotted eighth-sixteenth-note figure ♪♪ should be played as ♪♪. In this way, the ♪♪ rhythm in the right hand will fall together with the ♪♪ figure in the left hand.

**16.**

## Tremolo

The tremolo is a device frequently used in blues. It occurs in the form of quickly repeated notes, mostly thirds and octaves.

Sometimes the tremolo consists of whole chords, performed with one or both hands (a). Very often it is preceded by grace notes or slurs (b).

**17.**

## 18.

### Parallel Sixths (Left Hand)

The next exercise deals with sixths in the left hand. As in the previous exercises for the right hand, one should pay special attention to the smooth transition from one sixth to another and to the sounding of the two keys at precisely the same moment.

**19.**

**20.**

### Left-Hand Extension—Tenths

Physical limitations restrict the stretch of many hands. The present study will be helpful in the gradual extension of the grasp of the left hand, but it should not be practiced excessively.

**21.**

**22.**

## Compound Meter

Many blues are written in compound meter: $\frac{6}{8}$ or $\frac{12}{8}$. The subdivision of the eighth note into sixteenths and thirty-seconds creates problems in sight reading. The next exercise is a very helpful introduction to these meters. It contains two parts, A and B, which are identical with the exception that the first part is written in common meter, and the second in compound meter. The student is advised to compare the note values of the first section with those of the second, which should *sound* the same.

**23.** [A]

**24.**

**25.**

(bass solo)

**26.**

**27.**

**28.**

*rall.*

**29.**

**30.**

**31.**

60

**32.**

**33.**

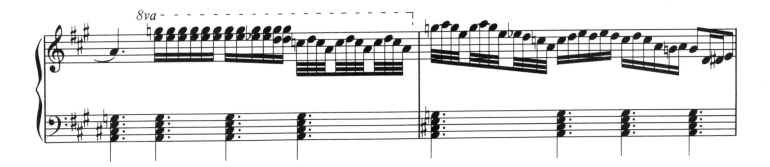